finding *joy* in the weeds

A CHRISTIAN DEVOTIONAL TO HELP WOMEN
THRIVE DURING CHALLENGING TIMES

Ashley Schubert

Copyright © 2024 – Ashley Schubert

Published by: Y'all Are Crazy Publishing

All rights reserved. No part of this publication may be reproduced, distributed, or transmitted in any form or by any means, without prior written permission from the publisher, except for brief quotations in critical reviews and certain other noncommercial uses permitted by copyright law.

1st Edition

Book cover design: Hilarie Gaston
Book layout design: Saqib Arshad

Printed in the United States of America

DISCLOSURE

Bible verses are taken from many Bible translations. I took the liberty to choose the translation that I felt best suited the devotional for the day. I am not a theologian and I did not go to seminary. I am an ordinary woman, likely just like you. I have used what God has given me to tell stories and encourage others along the way.

While these stories are all true, I meant no disrespect to any person(s) when writing them. God uses stories in order to impact others. Writing is my instrument so I hope that my life experiences can inspire my readers.

I believe God uses our authenticity, if we will let Him. People relate to those who are real. So, even though some of these stories are hard to tell, I pray they will make an impact because I am choosing to be raw and vulnerable.

I often give credit to friends along the way who encouraged me or told me something that stood out to me. Watch for special thanks to those friends in parenthesis as you read.

This devotional is meant to be read by women of all ages. I jokingly say it is for women and girls, ages 10-110. I do believe that is true! So whether you are tuning in at a young age, an old age, or somewhere in between, I pray you are blessed!

FROM THE AUTHOR

Before you begin this journey, I invite you to take a moment to reflect on your own journey and assess where you are right now. I ask that you say a prayer that your heart would be open to receive the message behind this devotional. As you turn each page, I pray it speaks to you directly.

Some stories are hard to share. But holding onto them does no one any good. So as you read, share what stood out to you with a friend, journal your thoughts, take time to process what spoke to you as you go.

All of my writing is God-inspired and written from a place of authenticity. I use my own stories and share the funny times and the really hard times with my readers. By doing so, I hope to capture the heart of those who may be going through the same things. God allows us to have gifts so that we may use them for His glory. He also guides us through both the good and the bad so that we may ultimately give Him glory. That's what I hope to do through my books, my writing and in my life. I hope this book blesses you and finds you right where you are. Whether it's on the mountaintop or down in the valley, I assure you, there is joy to be found, even in the weeds.

Ashley

CONTENTS

DAY 1 - Never Wanna Go Back...	1
DAY 2 - Losing Friends	3
DAY 3 - Totally Judas	5
DAY 4 - Just Another Picture to Burn	7
DAY 5 - The Story of the Pearl	9
DAY 6 - Multi-Passionate Mom	11
DAY 7 - Letting People Go	13
DAY 8 - Our Au Pair Adventure	15
DAY 9 - The World Keeps Putting Me In A Box	17
DAY 10 - Sit In the Suck	19
DAY 11 - Winning In the Long Run	21
DAY 12 - Big Battles and Little Ones	24
DAY 13 - God of the Hills and Valleys	26
DAY 14 - Build A Boat	28
DAY 15 - Finding Rest	30
DAY 16 - Nothin' Gonna Steal My Joy	32
DAY 17 - I Surrender All	34
DAY 18 - Move to Chandler!	36
DAY 19 - Sleeping on Air Mattresses In the Cold	38
DAY 20 - Give Yourself 24 hours	40
DAY 21 - Building a Home	42
DAY 22 - Chicken Butt	44
DAY 23 - Apologetics 101	46
DAY 24 - Praying the Satan out	48
DAY 25 - When Life Gives You Lemons...	50
DAY 26 - You Cannot Have a Testimony Without a Test	52
DAY 27 - Broken Bowls Lined With Gold	54
DAY 28 - Wrestling Day Jitters	56
DAY 29 - A'int That Just Like God?	58
DAY 30 - "You Look Happy"	60

Day 1

Never Wanna Go Back...

*The heart of man plans his way, but the L*ORD *establishes his steps.*

PROVERBS 16:9

I would not ever want to go back to where I was in the summer of 2022. In fact, you could not pay me to go back and relive it. If you told me you would give me $1,000,000 right now, I would tell you to keep your money. But if you were to ask me if it was worth it, I would say, undoubtedly, yes.

Sometimes God has to take you over a waterfall to make you into a river. A good friend of mine said this to me during one of the hardest times in my life (thank you, Sam). Can you envision those photos you have seen of a barrel going over Niagara Falls? Imagine you were inside that barrel. That is exactly how I felt. With rapids all around me and really no clear indication of how this might end, I felt that I had no other choice but to go over the waterfall and keep going.

They say God only gives the hard trials to those whom He knows can handle them. That may be true in some sense. But honestly, we cannot handle the hardest trials without God's help. Throughout the last year, after being shaken down to my core, I learned more than ever that God is the only thing I truly need. It really does not matter what happens to you. It matters how you respond and move forward.

After being taken down to Ground Zero, I was able to rebuild the way I wanted. And you know what? I discovered a leadership gift within myself, stronger than I had ever known before. I was able to develop a mission statement based on what I now knew to be true. And it attracted people who wanted the same thing! If I had not had to start over, I would have stayed in a comfortable place, in a place of complacency, where I was not happy. Instead, I went into an uncomfortable place and found happiness and a bright future!

> ### REFLECTION QUESTION
> Is comfort holding you back from your full potential?

Day 2

Losing Friends

A friend is always loyal.

PROVERBS 17:17

Is there anything worse than losing friendships? Like seriously, does anything hurt more than that? In addition to losing my business that I had built and grown over the last three years, I lost friendships that I had enjoyed for years as well - two friendships in particular. These friends had been the kind of friends who had walked beside me during hard times, lifted me up when I needed encouragement and I had poured myself into time and time again. They were the kind of friends I thought would be lifelong ones - but sadly, they were not meant to be that. Unfortunately, I had to learn that the hard way and feel all the pain that went along with it. Throughout that time, I had to rely on God's strength more than ever! I wondered time and time again if there was something wrong with me. Sometimes I still wonder about that, to be honest. But I have to hold onto the truth of scripture and not be afraid to make friendships moving forward, even though I have been hurt in the past. That, perhaps, is the most challenging thing of all. We want to guard our hearts from future pain. But, by doing that, we are blocking out the potential for future relationships, bonds and fun.

Whether we have been hurt in past relationships, be it friendships, romantic relationships or in family drama, we have to let it all go! We have to allow God to work in our hearts and transform our minds. The Bible says to pray for our enemies. My, what a challenge that is! By the way, I also read in Psalms that David prayed for God to "pour hot coals over his enemies' heads". Wow, David! I feel ya, buddy. I've felt that way a time or two in my life as well. If David prayed it, we can know there is grace for our human condition (haha)! We must forgive, give it to God and move on. Sometimes, that is easier said than done. It takes time. But ultimately, it is necessary in the healing process.

God never promises life will not give us more than we can handle. That is the point. Life will always give us more than we can handle. That is why we need a big God to walk with us in life's greatest storms and through life's greatest challenges. God is good, even when life is not.

REFLECTION QUESTION

Is a hurt from the past keeping you from moving forward? How can you let that hurt go, give it to God and move ahead in faith?

Day 3

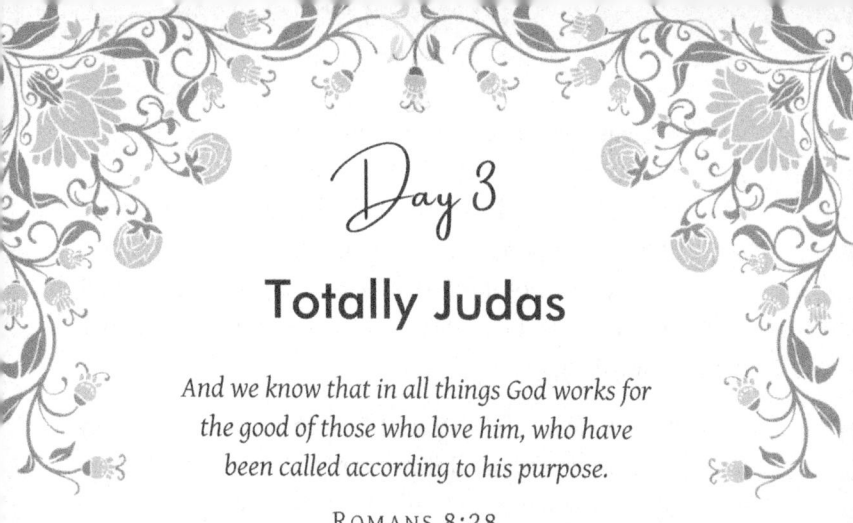

Totally Judas

*And we know that in all things God works for
the good of those who love him, who have
been called according to his purpose.*

ROMANS 8:28

Have you ever lost a friend? Not just an acquaintance, but a really close friend? I am convinced that nothing is more brutal than losing someone you once cared about. Someone you trusted, broke bread with, shared secrets with and who you thought would be in your life forever. Friends are hard to find, and as an adult, it is even harder. So to lose a friend is devastating - especially when you least expect it.

Do you think Jesus would have chosen Judas to be one of His 12 disciples if He had known Judas would betray Him? Since Jesus is God in the flesh, maybe He did know what Judas would eventually do. Or perhaps God did not make this known to Jesus when He was choosing His disciples. The disciples were not only his followers, they were His friends, His closest companions, His trusted ones.

When I think about friends who betrayed me, due to things beyond my control, it is so incredibly hurtful. It fills me with sadness to think about all the hurtful things that were done and said behind my back. I had a couple of these friends who turned their backs on me - friends I had gone on family vacations with, celebrated birthdays with, babysat my kids, shared amazing times with. Unbelievably, they chose to cut off our friendship and go along with the crowd. I have tried to justify their actions over time, but I still cannot process it. Truthfully, I do not need to understand why. Life is unfair and unpredictable. I can focus on the wrongs but they will never make it right.

Jesus knows how I felt. One of His best friends literally betrayed Him and handed Him over to be crucified. I am in no way comparing myself to Jesus or trying to comprehend how He felt. I am only comforted by the fact that He knows exactly how I felt. He was a human and felt real emotions. He was left with only a few people who believed in Him, who stood by Him at the cross, who mourned alongside Him. And that was enough. I choose to move forward in faith, believing that God will bring the right friendships along the way!

REFLECTION QUESTION

I believe that Jesus would have still befriended Judas if He had known the outcome. They had good times together, miraculous times even. If Jesus faced betrayal, why would I think that I won't?

Day 4

Just Another Picture to Burn

When you pass through the waters, I will be with you; And through the rivers, they shall not overflow you. When you walk through the fire, you shall not be burned, Nor shall the flame scorch you.

ISAIAH 43:2

I am not saying I have handled everything perfectly when it comes to the pain of the past. I am human also, with real emotions and feelings. And just like you, I am trying to figure it all out as I go along. But, I will tell you that burning something in a flame is therapeutic. When I was hurting but wanting desperately to move on, I decided to burn a piece of memorabilia from my past. It was a giant wooden key that I used to use in photos. It had the name of my prior company and it represented time spent, years spent, that I will never get back. I decided to throw it in the fire, turn on Taylor Swift's song *Picture To Burn* and let it go up in smoke. Please, you do not have to tell me it is not the Christian thing to do. I know it is not. But man, did it feel good. It was good for me to put an end to my past life and realize it was never going to be the same again. It was part of my healing process and I needed it.

Since that time, I have moved past the "anger" stage and am in a much better place. I have sat through church services, cried, written and forgiven. Rather than living in that anger I felt when I burned the wooden key, I now feel peace. Here is the thing - anger and revenge will never bring us peace and freedom. Only God can do that. We have to allow Him access into our life to transform our minds and our hearts.

I have also realized that time is never wasted. Sure, I can never get those years back that I spent. But I learned so much during those years! They taught me about systems, processes and how to be a good leader. I am in such a better place now because of what I learned then. God will restore what you thought were wasted years. As it is written in scripture: "I will restore to you the years that the swarming locust has eaten, the hopper, the destroyer, and the cutter, my great army, which I sent among you. You shall eat in plenty and be satisfied, and praise the name of the LORD your God, who has dealt wondrously with you." Joel 2:25-27

REFLECTION QUESTION

What do you need to do to process hurt so that you can move forward in peace?

Day 5

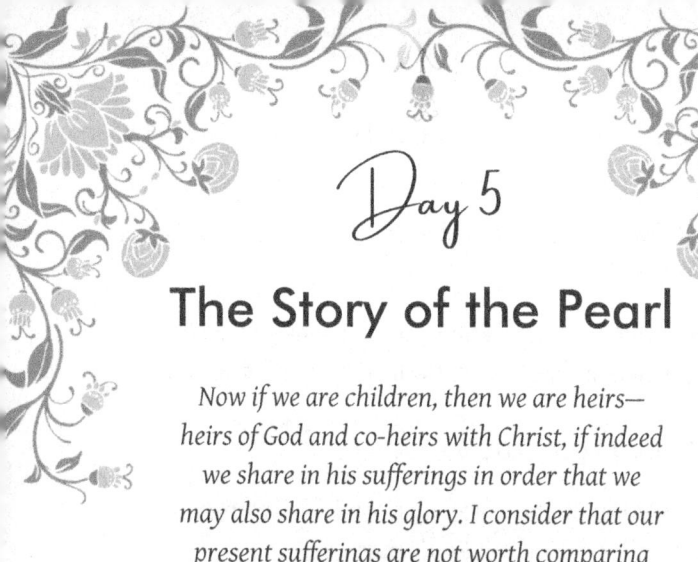

The Story of the Pearl

*Now if we are children, then we are heirs—
heirs of God and co-heirs with Christ, if indeed
we share in his sufferings in order that we
may also share in his glory. I consider that our
present sufferings are not worth comparing
with the glory that will be revealed in us.*

ROMANS 8:17-18

My friend sent me this story and I thought it was beautiful. (Thank you, Becky!)

Did you know? An oyster that has not been wounded in any way does not produce pearls?

A pearl is a healed wound.

Pearls are the product of pain, the result of a foreign or unwanted substance entering the oyster, such as a parasite or a grain of sand.

The inside of an oyster shell is a shiny substance called "nacre".

When a grain of sand enters, the nacre cells go to work and cover the grain of sand with layers and more layers to protect the defenseless body from the oyster. As a result, a beautiful pearl is formed!

The more pearls, the more valuable. God never allows pain without a purpose.

What if your greatest ministry to others comes out of your greatest hurt?

The hard things we may be going through now are really nothing in comparison to the glory that will be revealed in us later.

> **REFLECTION QUESTION**
>
> In what area of your life have you been wounded? How can it be used for God's purpose?

Day 6

Multi-Passionate Mom

A wife of noble character who can find? She is worth far more than rubies.

PROVERBS 31:10

I often refer to women who do it all as "unicorns". We are out there, but we are not common.

I have come to the conclusion that I do not need to have ONLY one passion in life. For the first decade of my career, I became hyper-focused on real estate. I was good at it and able to earn a really good income for my family, better than I had ever dreamed possible! Once I hit year 10, I started my own brokerage and learned that I still love real estate but it is not my only passion.

Over the years, I have discovered that I am really passionate about building businesses, helping and supporting women in their journeys and managing the daily workings of a business. I love leadership! That has allowed me to run several businesses, not just be a Realtor. Discovering that I do not just have to be one thing is very freeing! It has taken me a while to get my new elevator pitch down. But now I can start it with "I am a multi-passionate business owner"...and be really proud of it.

In addition to running multiple businesses, I am also an author, speaker and podcast host. I enjoy the challenge of writing, the exhilaration of speaking, and the excitement of podcasting. I love it all. And that's okay!

I am also a mom of many. I love being home with them every evening, baking cookies, getting them on the bus each morning, taking field trips to the zoo and more! I love being a Mom.

All of these things are okay because God created me with a unique skill set and personality. He created all of us that way. Because of that, He knew what our passions would be, what we would be good at and enjoy doing. Most importantly, He knew who we would impact by doing these things. Instead of sitting around and worrying about what all we do, let's embrace it! And let's use it all for God's glory!

> ### REFLECTION QUESTION
> Are you holding onto one title when you could be embracing more of who you are?

Day 7

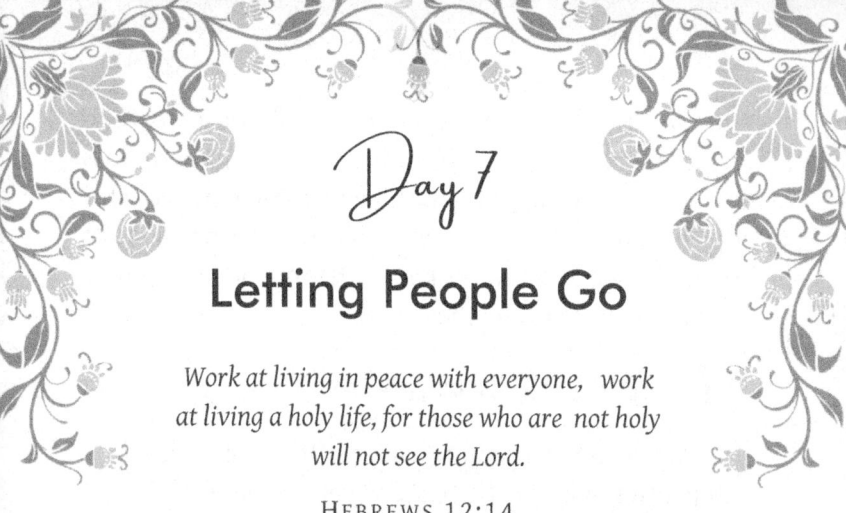

Letting People Go

Work at living in peace with everyone, work at living a holy life, for those who are not holy will not see the Lord.

HEBREWS 12:14

Sometimes it is hard to say goodbye. Well honestly, it is usually hard to say goodbye. Sometimes we have to let people go in our lives, in more ways than one. I had a good house cleaner that I liked; she helped with groceries and laundry and such. And I liked her a lot. She was just not the best for the role and I needed a better fit. When I decided it was best to let her go, I was kind, yet clear. Throughout the years, I have definitely learned that "clear is kind". My business coach often says that. Boy, how true it is! When you beat around the bushes and sugarcoat things, there is confusion and hurt. I have definitely handled this the wrong way over the years, more than once. We learn as we grow!

In this instance, even though I was sad to let that person go, it opened up the job role to someone new. Coincidentally, I had someone reach out to me on Facebook asking if I ever needed any help around my house. God is not a God of coincidences! She was able to start soon after I let my last one go and it was a peaceful and smooth transition.

When we are clear with our motives, it allows us space to separate and exit peacefully and with grace. There does not need to be yelling and hurt feelings. There is room for peaceful goodbyes. It is very important to never burn bridges because you never know what opportunities may be awaiting just around the corner.

> ### REFLECTION QUESTION
>
> Do you need to let someone in your life go in order to step into something better? Can you do that with intentions of being "clear" and "kind"?

Day 8

Our Au Pair Adventure

He will once again fill your mouth with laughter and your lips with shouts of joy.

JOB 8:21

I always wanted to write about our adventure with our Au Pair, but I never got around to doing it. So this serves as a short synopsis of that journey.

We decided to get an Au Pair to help our family and it was a year-long contract. An Au Pair is someone who comes from another country to serve a United States family with childcare and household needs. Ours came from Columbia and needless to say, the United States was a much different world than the one she was used to! She spoke English, but not well. She could speak it better than she could understand it. Many times, she would respond with "yes" but she did not understand what we were trying to tell her.

We had so many funny experiences because when you mix two cultures together, it can lead to chaos! On several occasions, she loaded the dishwasher with dishes and used Dawn dish soap instead of dishwasher detergent, causing it to overflow with bubbles. One day I walked in and she was dipping a hotdog bun into her coffee for breakfast (yuck). Another time, I saw her dumping sugar into the baby's milk bottle because she thought he needed it to be sweet for him to drink it (yikes)! The funny stories could go on and on. We taught her how to drive, helped her get a license and experienced her bad driving skills in the front row seat. One day she ran into our gate box and dented the van! It was quite the experience having someone from another country live with us. The pot of grease was something she cooked with daily and kept in the cabinet to fry all her favorite foods, including plantains. She liked to play soccer with the kids, and honestly acted more like a kid herself, rather than a 26-year-old woman. Cultural differences can be huge and they certainly were in our case!

Unfortunately, the fit was not right for us and we were able to get out of our contract. It is an experience that was frustrating at times but now we can look back on it and laugh. We have some funny stories and experiences to share. Most importantly, you never know if something is going to work until you try it! So, do not be afraid to try something new. Even if it does not work out, experiences can still come out of it along the way!

> *REFLECTION QUESTION*
>
> What have you been afraid to try because you're afraid it might not work out?

Day 9

The World Keeps Putting Me In A Box

Blessed is the one who does not walk in step with the wicked or stand in the way that sinners take or sit in the company of mockers, but whose delight is in the law of the LORD, and who meditates on his law day and night. That person is like a tree planted by streams of water, which yields its fruit in season and whose leaf does not wither— whatever they do prospers.

PSALM 1:1-3

The world likes to tell us we have to choose. "You must be this in order to be this", they say. The world seems to want to make us choose one thing. When I started speaking professionally, I was sometimes misunderstood. It was like groups did not know how to take me. Yes, I was a Christian woman who had children, who always worked and made an income, and yes, I loved Jesus. I felt out of place sometimes, discouraged at other times. Sometimes, I did not know what genre I truly fit into.

I wanted to preach the gospel and share Bible verses, encouragement and biblical teaching. But I was also a business professional with great success in the real estate industry. I was also a mom who could speak on the struggles and joys of parenthood. So which group should I speak to? I could speak on business, motherhood and faith. But I refused to be put into a corner. Yes, I was all of these things and still am! But I can be all three at once. I don't have to be confined to one thing. The trinity is real (God was three-in-one), come on now!

God made us to shine! Just like the children's song goes, "This little light of mine, I'm gonna let it shine. Let it shine, let it shine, let it shine". If God created us uniquely and individually, he can create a lane for us as well. We are not made to be put into a box. Just maybe we can cross barriers and reach people in various groups along the way! And just like the famous children's author, Dr. Suess said, "Why fit in when you were born to stand out?" So, stand out, friend! It's your time to shine!

> ### REFLECTION QUESTION
> How can you use the talents God has given you?

Day 10

Sit In the Suck

I know the plans I have for you. Plans to give you hope and a future.

JEREMIAH 29:11

During one of the hardest times of my life, I felt like I was losing everything I had worked so hard to build. I felt betrayed, I felt unseen and under-appreciated. I was unsure of the future - and it was a scary time, to be sure. I wrote this during that time:

I know that God is growing me and has great plans for my future. I know that we grow the most during the most difficult times. Going through them is just no fun at all. It's overwhelming, frustrating and hard on the heart. It's excruciatingly painful, gut-wrenching and just plain sad. I have to believe that God has bigger plans for me and will bring me out better on the other side.

One of my friends says, "Don't be afraid to sit in the suck for a while" (thank you, Jantzen). I feel like that's exactly what I'm doing - sitting "in the suck". And it is just as bad as it sounds.

While that is difficult to read because I wrote that during a very low point, it is truly amazing to see how far God has brought me! He had a plan for my pain and a purpose behind it. While going through hard times is rarely enjoyable - it is inevitable. God literally knew the hard times we would go through before they happened. He never promised there would not be pain. He promised He would never leave us or forsake us. He promised to walk beside us in the pain and be our constant companion along the way.

I encourage you to journal if you're going through a hard time. It helps to get words on paper for how you are feeling. It is also cool to look back over the journal entries as time has passed. I can see God's hand on my life and how He carried me through the rough waters. Without Him, my hope would have been limited. Because of Him, I can have joy, even in the weeds.

> ### REFLECTION QUESTION
>
> Looking back on hard times, think about how you felt then and how you feel now. How have you seen the faithfulness of God?

Day 11

Winning In the Long Run

> *"Consider it pure joy, my brothers and sisters, whenever you face trials of many kinds, because you know that the testing of your faith produces perseverance. Let perseverance finish its work so that you may be mature and complete, not lacking anything."*
>
> JAMES 1:2-4

Do you know what it's like to lose almost every friend that you have? I do. Do you know what it is like for people to turn their back on you in a single day while you are left picking up the pieces? I do.

I am sure most of us can say we have experienced these things. If we are honest, we can say we have experienced them while not wanting to experience them. Once you get past the fog of the hurt, though, you start to see the light on the other side. It makes you more grateful for the friends you do have. The friends who stepped beside you and never left. The people who cheered you on, even if those people were ones you never thought would be in your cheering section!

Throughout my experiences, I have learned not to take anyone for granted. To cherish the ones that are in my life and by my side. I also learned how to dig in and work really hard and strategically toward my goals! One thing to remember is that today's supposed failure can set you up for tomorrow's guaranteed success!

I read a quote this week that said "What seems overwhelming now will be your testimony later". There is a lot of truth in that statement and it goes back to the truth that we cannot have a testimony without a test. Sometimes we do not want our testimony. We beg God to give us another. But our testimony is ours for a reason. So we can overcome and then tell people about how God helped us every step of the way! I love this famous poem:

One night I dreamed a dream.
As I was walking along the beach with my Lord.
Across the dark sky flashed scenes from my life.
For each scene, I noticed two sets of footprints in the sand,
One belonging to me and one to my Lord.

After the last scene of my life flashed before me,
I looked back at the footprints in the sand.
I noticed that at many times along the path of my life,
especially at the very lowest and saddest times,
there was only one set of footprints.

This really troubled me, so I asked the Lord about it.
"Lord, you said once I decided to follow you,
You'd walk with me all the way.
But I noticed that during the saddest and most troublesome times of my life,
there was only one set of footprints.
I don't understand why, when I needed You the most, You would leave me."

He whispered, "My precious child, I love you and will never leave you

Never, ever, during your trials and testings.
When you saw only one set of footprints,
It was then that I carried you."

(Written by Mary Stevenson)

> ### REFLECTION QUESTION
>
> What is God carrying you through right now? How might that just be your testimony later?

Day 12

Big Battles and Little Ones

But whatever former things were gains to me [as I thought then], these things [once regarded as advancements in merit] I have come to consider as loss [absolutely worthless] for the sake of Christ [and the purpose which He has given my life].

PHILIPPIANS 3:7

The Lord is my refuge and strength - a very present help when trouble comes.

When I don't know what to do, I will look to you, Lord.

This is a prayer we can say often in motherhood and in life. We often think about God helping us during big battles (and He does) but He also wants to help us in the little valleys as well. On hard days, when our kids are driving us batty, when we are cleaning up messes for the hundredth time some days, when we don't think we can handle hearing the words "Mom, Momma, Mommy" one more time - He is there with us too. With six kids, I cannot tell you how many times each day I hear those words. It is literally countless, endless and overwhelming at times. Sometimes I do not know how I will make it through the day, and then I look up and it is only 9:00 AM. It is funny because it is true. Can you relate? Bless.

It is easy to ask God for help in times we are in the big battles. That makes sense. We desperately need Him. We should seek Him during big battles. But we can also seek Him in desperate times and on hard days, during daily setbacks and moments when we feel like we do not measure up. Sometimes the valleys can feel just as overwhelming as the big battles when we are not sure how we can possibly "win". I have felt like such a losing Mom on some hard days, a useless leader at the office on others and an imposter in my profession on my worst days. But, thank goodness I am not who others say I am. I am who God says I am. And He says this - I am chosen. He chose me to be right where I am for the people He put before me - and he chose you too, friend. You are chosen, you are loved and with God's help, you are equipped.

As we look to Him for strength, may we feel equipped to handle the struggles and count them as gain as we allow Christ to work through us.

> ### REFLECTION QUESTION
>
> What's your big battle? How can you view the struggles as hidden blessings?

Day 13

God of the Hills and Valleys

The man of God came up and told the king of Israel, "This is what the LORD says: 'Because the Arameans think the LORD is a god of the hills and not a god of the valleys, I will deliver this vast army into your hands, and you will know that I am the LORD.'

1 KINGS 20:28

This is the title of one of my favorite songs. It's by Tauren Wells and it plays on the radio often. I recently spoke at a women's conference in Arizona and when they asked me what song I wanted as my "walk-out song", I quickly decided this one would be mine. The chorus says, "You're God of the hills and valleys. I am not alone". These words keep me grounded and help me remember this truth - God has been and will always be with me in both.

In the hills - on those mountaintop moments when I am winning, succeeding, feel amazing - He is there. May I never forget to humble myself so that I do not forget that it was God who got me to those moments. I love to sit in those moments as I imagine God standing beside me as I embrace the feeling of happiness and fulfillment. And then...there are times when the valley seems so overwhelming and it threatens to swallow me up. God is with me in those times too. He is still standing beside me. In fact, He never left. The second line in the chorus says "I am not alone". That truth means that I am not alone on the hilltop or in the valley. What a blessing it is to have a friend who will never leave, never betray us and that we don't have to worry about abandoning us. He never will. Throughout the course of my life, I have lost friendships and relationships and it has caused me to be rather guarded at times. I am still working on my own mindset through this and praying that God softens my heart as I continue to heal. It hurts when friends leave, right? Thankfully, God will never leave and He is the constant friend that we always need by our side.

He is there on the hilltops so don't forget to thank Him when you are up there! He is also with you on the valley floors (praise!) so do not forget to talk to Him down there either. I promise you, you will experience both in your life. Never forget, you are not alone.

> ### REFLECTION QUESTION
>
> Write down your story of how God is the one on the hilltop and in the valley. He's beside you. Your story can help others!

Day 14

Build A Boat

"When I shut up the heavens so that there is no rain, or command locusts to devour the land or send a plague among my people, if my people, who are called by my name, will humble themselves and pray and seek my face and turn from their wicked ways, then I will hear from heaven, and I will forgive their sin and will heal their land.."

2 CHRONICLES 7:13-14

When we had lived in our new community for about a year, I felt very strongly that I needed to open an office space in our new town. It would require more money, effort and time to be sure. And time was something I did not have. In order to open another real estate location, I knew I legally needed another broker on staff. The problem is, those are not just lying around waiting. I prayed and asked God to provide someone if I was supposed to do this. And lo and behold, a friend called me the next day and said she wanted to move to my brokerage. And by golly, she had a broker's license. Isn't God funny like that? We opened up a third location quickly after, started a new location and began the hard work on demolition, renovating and marketing!

We also opened it up to serve as an event venue; So I am pursuing another passion! Helping people gather to celebrate life's biggest occasions! It has been fun and challenging, yet amazing!

The work is still there, it is still hard some days and the challenge is real. But when we build a boat, God can send the rain.

You're the map, You're my compass
You help me navigate the currents underneath
Take the lead, I surrender
Every word You say is gonna come true
You will lead me to the promised land
Everything You say is gonna happen
Even though I haven't seen it yet
I will build a boat in the sand where they say it never rains
I will stand up in faith, I'll do anything it takes
With Your wind in my sails, Your love never fails or fades
I'll build a boat in the desert place
And when the flood and the water starts to rise, yeah
I'll ride the storm 'cause I got You by my side
With Your wind in my sails, Your love never fails or fades
I'll build a boat, so let it rain
I'll build a boat, so let it rain

Song by Colton Dixon

> ### REFLECTION QUESTION
>
> How can you "build a boat" today? God will send the rain when he is ready.

Day 15

Finding Rest

Come to me, all who labor and are heavy laden, and I will give you rest.

MATTHEW 11:28

Rest is a strange thing. We all know it is essential. Yet, do we really value it? Our society certainly does not. But God created six days to work and one day to rest. So if it is important to God, it should be important to us. It's something I struggle with because I am a busy bee. I like to be active, going and accomplishing things!

I took more time to rest during my last maternity leave than I ever had before. Maternity leave is a weird concept because as we know, moms do not really get to rest,especially when we have multiple kiddos or when we also have businesses to run or homes to care for or husbands to love. Moms do not get a chance to truly get a break very often. I had the baby on a Tuesday and good golly, fall break began that Thursday! That means the kids were out of school for four days and I was bringing home a newborn. I took the extra hospital day this time and I gave myself 48 hours in the hospital (I usually get out of there at the 24-hour mark.) Staying an extra day allowed me to rest, let someone else bring me meals so that I could focus on myself and the baby. My husband left to go home and sleep. He laughs because I say that my hospital is like a vacation to me. Someone brings me food and checks in on me regularly. It is quiet and I can just soak in the silence. Can I get an amen, Mamas? I physically rested. And it felt amazing.

Once I got home, real life began! But with it, I realized I needed to take it easy on myself. More time sitting with my feet up. More time snuggling my newborn. More time reading books to my toddlers. More time engaging with my big kids. That was a sweet time and one I can look back on with fondness.

Rest does not just need to happen when we are physically in the hospital. It needs to happen regularly, just as God commanded it. The Sabbath Day is part of the Ten Commandments, you know. That means, getting a good night's sleep, first of all. It means attending church on Sundays, fellowshipping with other believers, spending time with family and friends and reflecting on God's goodness. Rest means something different to each of us. It should be an essential part of our rhythm. In case you were wondering, I am still working on that as well.

> ### REFLECTION QUESTION
>
> Do you need rest? Physically, emotionally? How can you incorporate rest into your rhythm?

Day 16

Nothin' Gonna Steal My Joy

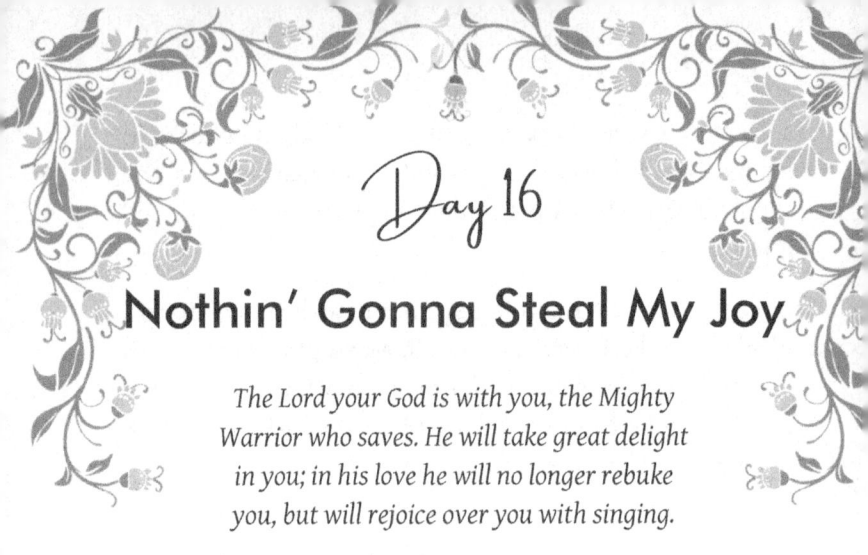

The Lord your God is with you, the Mighty Warrior who saves. He will take great delight in you; in his love he will no longer rebuke you, but will rejoice over you with singing.

ZEPHANIAH 3:1

Imagine this song playing...."There ain't nothin' gonna steal my joy...No, there ain't nothin' gonna steal my joyyyy..." (cue the "Old Church Choir" by Zach Williams).

Along with obstacles we may face in work, friendships, life and everything that comes with it, we are also part of a family. And with that comes challenges of its own. I have a husband, 6 children, a home, a ranch, 40 cows, 20 goats, 30 sheep and a partridge in a pear tree. Just kidding on that last part; I despise birds. I am just painting the picture for you of how chaotic life can be most of the time.

As I drove home one day, I sang that Zach Williams song. In that moment, everything was calm and bright. My car was happy and at peace. But, after that, reality set in.

For me, it often happens once I arrive home after a full day of work. Work makes me feel fueled, rejuvenated and optimistic. I'm good at working. Once I arrive home, the chaos begins and I wonder where that joy went that I felt just a few minutes ago. The house may be messy with toys and crumbs smashed into the rug. I must then make a choice. Take a deep breath, say "Lord, help me show grace" and smile. Or I could get upset, make everyone clean and be a drill sergeant. I've done this. I've learned that fuming and getting upset with my kids and husband really does not help anything. However, setting clear expectations does. I can say something to my family like "When I get home, this is what I expect to see". More often than not, when I set those clear expectations, they happen. Without expectations, there are no boundaries.

Dwelling on failures and having unrealistic expectations of others is pointless. Focusing on clear expectations and maintaining joy is within our control. What we allow our minds to consume, believe and dwell on becomes our mood. Our mood becomes our outlook and our outlook becomes our heart.

> ### REFLECTION QUESTION
>
> How can you set clear expectations to create more joy in your life?

Day 17

I Surrender All

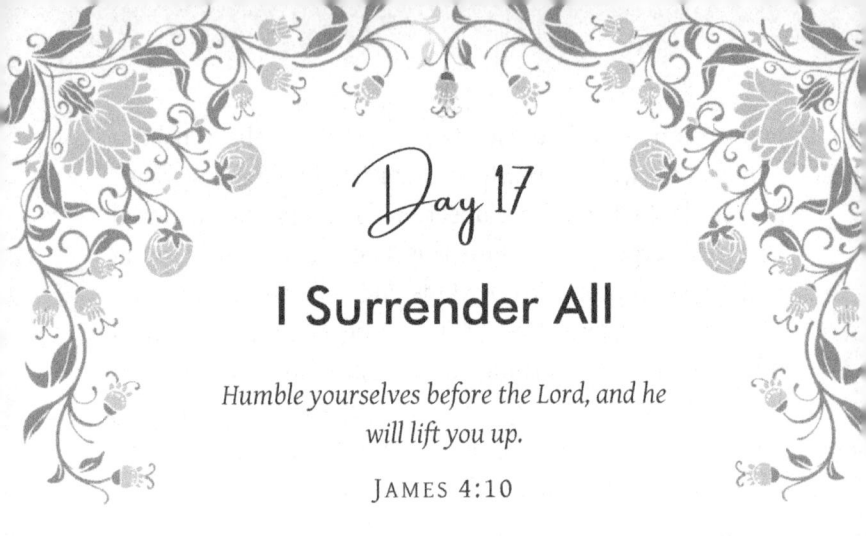

Humble yourselves before the Lord, and he will lift you up.

JAMES 4:10

I do not have any tattoos. I am scared of needles and do not like shots, blood work or anything to do with sharp objects entering my body. Granted, I have had 6 children and been poked and prodded along the way. But in that regard, I knew it was worth the pain to bring a new life into the world! With a tattoo, I cannot yet bring myself to bear that pain. However, if I were to get a tattoo, it would say this "I surrender all". Not only because I love the lyrics to the song, but also because I believe it is the only way to truly live! As I have grown (and aged) and matured, I have learned that the only way to live for Jesus is to give our lives to Him. That means dying to our flesh and giving him our hearts, futures and our lives fully.

When people ask me how I take risks, start new things, balance it all, I reply "God does it. I just keeping saying 'yes'!" When we live with hands wide open, it's amazing what God can do in us and through us. He cares about us and wants to work through us, if we will allow Him to do so! It is a conscious choice to surrender. God cannot do his work completely unless we surrender. And by doing so, we give Him control over our lives, our futures and our course.

Hymn:

All to Jesus I surrender, all to Him I freely give;
I will ever love and trust Him, in His presence daily live.
I surrender all, I surrender all.
All to thee, my blessed savior, I surrender all.

> ### REFLECTION QUESTION
>
> How can you surrender all to Christ so you can fully live?

Day 18

Move to Chandler!

Trust in the LORD with all your heart and lean not on your own understanding; in all your ways submit to him, and he will make your paths straight.

PROVERBS 3:5-6

I woke up bright and early one Saturday morning and felt God tell me "Open up your computer and look at homes in Chandler". What in the world? I did not even really know where this place was located. Let alone, anything about it. But being a Realtor, it was easy for me to pull up properties and see what was available. I quickly found a handful of homes to look at and woke up my husband. "Babe, we need to go look at houses in Chandler today!" I am sure he was confused, but he is used to my crazy shenanigans and has learned to trust me when I tell him where God is leading. Thankfully, he agreed to go and we saw a few homes that day. I walked into one which needed a lot of updating. It had yucky floors, blue carpets, dirty walls and each bathroom was a different color. When I say different I mean, one was blue complete with blue sinks, toilet and bathtub! The others were green and yellow I believe. This house was gross and in need of a full renovation. I looked at my husband and said "We need to buy this house because our family is going to live in it!" Now, keep in mind, we lived in a beautiful home on a large acreage and we were happy. We were simply searching for investment properties that we could rent out for our investment portfolio. We were not looking for a new place to live. But God.

My husband agreed that the home was a good purchase at a good price in a great location. We signed the contract and ended up purchasing it. Our plan was to renovate it and then list it "for rent". However, the Lord is true to his word. When we listen to the Holy Spirit, He directs us and leads us down paths we cannot understand. A few months later, we found our dream land in the city of Chandler. We moved into that little rental home that I sensed our family would live in someday. And we currently live in that property while we build our new home on our land. When we listen to God's leading and have the faith to step out when things do not make sense, he can do the impossible.

> ### REFLECTION QUESTION
>
> How can you trust God even when it doesn't make sense?

Day 19

Sleeping on Air Mattresses In the Cold

And God is able to bless you abundantly, so that in all things at all times, having all that you need, you will abound in every good work.

2 CORINTHIANS 9:8

When we moved into our little in-between home in town, a lot changed for us. We downsized by more than half and went from 40 acres to 0.25 acres with a backyard. The kids faced a major transition as they had never lived in a neighborhood (that they could remember). It was an interesting time. Not to mention, it was January and it was cold.

We ordered a new mattress and got rid of our old one. So we slept on air mattresses on the floor, waiting until the new ones came in. Did I mention we had a three-month old? Well we did. So, most nights, he slept on that air mattress right beside me. The house we were living in had not been lived in for years and though it had been recently renovated, there were growing pains to work through. The heating unit was blowing dirt from the vents so instead of central heat, we used space heaters to stay warm. The plumbing kept clogging up because the lines were old and the pipes were jagged. So instead of flushing toilet paper, we had to throw the paper away in plastic bags. One night, our shower flooded and the wood floors buckled. There were too many instances to count and on more than one occasion, we questioned our sanity. We had moved from a beautiful home to a small home that just didn't function. Oh yeah, with five kids and a newborn. After months of living in the house and lots of repair calls, the kinks began to work themselves out. We got the house up to standard and were able to enjoy the tiny home.

Here is the thing. We knew God asked us to move. He made a way so that we could. But it wasn't comfortable or convenient. Here's what I know. God doesn't call us to do hard things. He calls us to do impossible things. Even in the uncomfortable, God makes a way. Even when you're sleeping on cold air mattresses and dealing with flooding showers.

> ### REFLECTION QUESTION
>
> What discomfort are you going through now? God can bless you through the hard times. Pray for that today.

Day 20

Give Yourself 24 hours

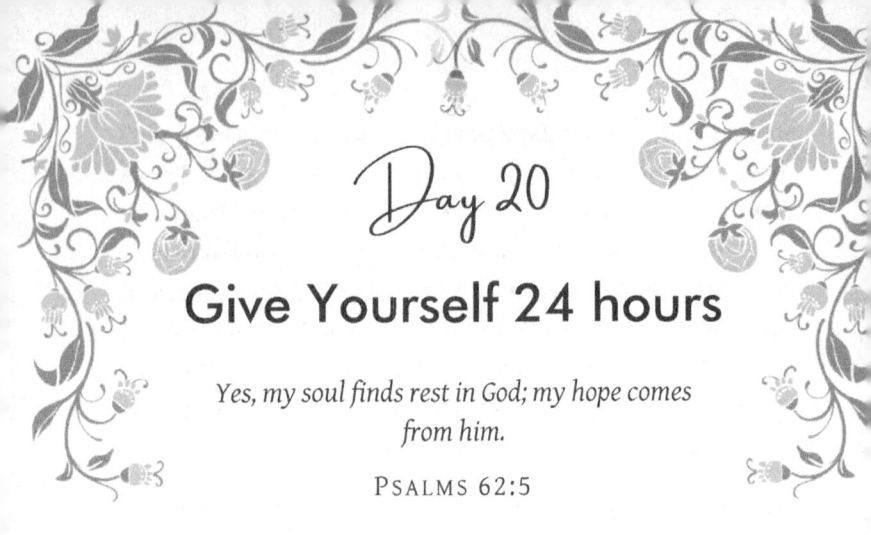

Yes, my soul finds rest in God; my hope comes from him.

PSALMS 62:5

My rule of thumb when things go wrong is what I lovingly refer to as the "24-hour rule". I give myself 24 hours to be sad, angry, bitter, you name it. I allow myself to feel the emotions, talk to my husband about it, get it all out, journal and then go to bed. The next day, I get up and say "Well, that was unexpected. Now what am I going to do about it?" (Of course, I'm not referring to times when we need months, years, a lifetime to grieve, like the loss of a loved one.) I am referring to times when the path we are on is not what we expected and we have to rebound. I believe what sets us apart as victors is how quickly we can fail and then move on from it! Sometimes, the failure may be our fault, fully or partially, and other times it may be completely out of our control. What matters is how we take the next step forward. Coco Chanel said "Success is most often achieved by those who don't know that failure is inevitable."

When I was going through a particularly difficult time, feeling betrayed and hurt, I did not see a bright day in sight. A friend wrote me a nice card (Thank you, Jeff) and this is what it said:

Ashley,

I heard about the mutiny. That brought back so many emotions still inside me when that happened to us. When we pour into other people, help them, coach them up, love on their families...and they disregard that for selfish reasons, it's hard to take. But, I will tell you that now, I know it was for the better. The front side of the miracle is really hard to endure, but the backside is beautiful. God has bigger things for you...get ready!

The letter meant so much to me. Looking back now, I can tell you it is true. I can see the blessings on the other side! It takes a lot of grit to push through when times are hard and you just want to be bitter. But being bitter does not set us up for a brighter future. It keeps us stuck in a place of bitterness, where our hearts can get hard. Needless to say, that's not a place we want to be. Moving past the hard isn't easy, of course. But, it's necessary. So, give yourself a day to "sit in the suck" and then wake up with a new motive - "What are you going to do about it?"

REFLECTION QUESTION

Can you write a letter to a friend to encourage them right now? I challenge you to do it!

Day 21

Building a Home

May the God of hope fill you with all joy and peace as you trust in him, so that you may overflow with hope by the power of the Holy Spirit.

ROMANS 15:13

We had been working on our house plans for well over a year. We were finally to the point to submit everything for final approval and push the green light! I could already see our beautiful home on the hilltop! And then...bam! We were hit with final figures from our builder that the home was not going to be a reality (at least not at the price we wanted). We decided to part ways with the builder and the architect at that point. We then took on the task of starting over. And boy, did that stink! We took a day to be mad, upset and heartbroken. And then woke up the next day and said "Well that stinks. Now what are we going to do about it?"

They say building a house together can test your marriage like nothing else can. Maybe that is true. But it can also bring you closer together as a couple, closer in your relationship with God and reliant on wisdom from above like never before.

Here is the thing: God knows what is ahead for us. He knows the struggles we will face. He knows the objections we will get and he knows how we will overcome them! So whatever comes our way, we can know that God already has it all worked out anyway!

I told a friend recently that I was no longer going to be controlled by worry, doubt or fear. I'm going to live with hands wide open for whatever God has for me! Sometimes, that means saying "yes" when it makes no sense. Sometimes, it means saying "bye". Often, it means having faith when no one else around you does. Always, it means surrendering to God's will. Like I told my friend, "I'm just a vessel". God loves to use vessels.

> *REFLECTION QUESTION*
>
> How can you be a vessel for the Lord? Do you need to let go of fear in order to live in this way?

Day 22

Chicken Butt

Praise the LORD! He is good.
God's love never fails.
Praise the God of all gods.
God's love never fails.
Praise the Lord of lords.
God's love never fails.

PROVERBS 136:1-3

Boys are odd creatures. If you have ever had little boys, you will understand this. When little boys reach about the age of 3, they find it funny to say the word "butt" or "poop". They think those two words are the most hilarious thing they have ever heard! One evening as we were leaving church, we stood outside chatting with the pastor. We had walked to church that evening because we lived very close by at the time. We had the baby in the stroller and all the other kids walked alongside us. As we smiled and waved goodbye to the pastor, we started walking away. Before we were fully out of hearing range, our three-year-old turned around to the pastor, smiled and waved and loudly said "bye bye, chicken butt"! When I tell you I about died, I did. I wanted to crawl underneath a rock. Thankfully, the pastor just smiled and waved. I am only hoping he did not hear the chicken butt remark (although I do not know how he could have missed it). Kids can make us so proud in one moment, while making us want to hide from embarrassment the next.

I wonder if God ever feels that way about us? It's easy to imagine God being proud of us as his children when we make good choices, witness to a friend, sing praise songs at church. But what about when we make a wrong turn, say something we should not have, do something we will later regret. The truth is, God is never embarrassed by us. We knew what we were going to do before we did it, because, well He is God. But he also has grace on us as he knows our human nature. He is a proud parent who loves us unconditionally. I am thankful for that even when I do things that are sinful, embarrassing or silly.

REFLECTION QUESTION

When have you felt you embarrassed yourself, God or your family? How has God shown you that he loves you unconditionally?

Day 23

Apologetics 101

For everything there is a season, and a time for every matter under heaven.

ECCLESIASTES 3:1

When I was pregnant with our sixth child, I thought it was a great idea to go back to school to get another Master's degree. Granted, when I received my first Master's, I was married but had no children, a 9-5 job and no other real commitments. I remember it being pretty easy to go to class, stay caught up on homework, breeze through 36 hours and knock it out in a cool year-and-a-half. Fast forward....10 years. With a home, hubby, six children and several businesses to run, this time around looked a little bit different. I was maxed out and still trying to fit school work inside the little amount of margin that I actually had. I was typing essays while nursing a baby on one side. I was staying up late to complete assignments and using Sunday afternoons to catch up on homework. Needless to say, my plate was too full.

I am not good at admitting I am in over my head. I am worse at admitting I should not finish something I started. Maybe it is embarrassment, maybe it is pride. It is likely a combination of both. Nevertheless, I knew I needed to put a "pause" on this secondary degree. So I did. I decided that when I did pursue this degree, I wanted to do so fully and with an open mind and margin to really grasp and grow in God's word. I needed to give my dedication to really reading and studying. Not just getting by, but feeling proud of my work.

So instead of saying "I'm done", I said "I'm pausing". Maybe I will pick it up in a few years or maybe it will be a decade before I want to look at another textbook. But, I completed 9 hours and only have 27 hours to go. In God's timing, I will come back to it. But for now, I can smile and say "that's just not my season". Life comes in seasons and that's a beautiful thing if we allow it to be.

> ### REFLECTION QUESTION
>
> What do you need to put a "pause" on right now and save for another season?

Day 24

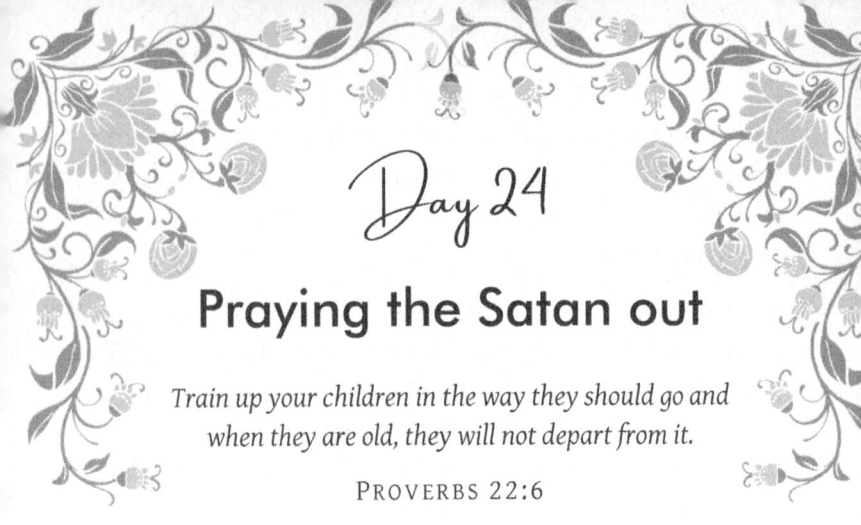

Praying the Satan out

Train up your children in the way they should go and when they are old, they will not depart from it.

PROVERBS 22:6

My 4th son at 5 years old is very strong-willed. And when I say "very", I mean it. I tell my husband that perhaps we should not have named him after the "lion chaser" of the Bible. His namesake literally defied those around him to show his strength and power given to him. As my son entered Pre-K, we were optimistic as he was making friends easily and progressing with ease in his schoolwork. But then the attitude began. Defiance against his dad and I were very evident. He would look me in the eye and say "no". Nothing seemed to work. Sitting in time-out, the old-fashioned whooping, nothing. He didn't care if he hurt our feelings. He didn't cry - didn't even show emotion. One day after school, he pushed his little brother down to the ground. I asked him to help him up, give him a hug and say "sorry". Of course, he just smirked and said no. I tried over and over again. I did all the forms of punishment. I was at the end of my rope with this kid. So, on a particularly challenging afternoon after school, I said "that's it, I'm opening the Bible!" I literally opened it to the first passage I came to and began reading. I think it was Psalm 1. He stared at me in disbelief as I just read, with intention, passion and even a few tears. I then put my hand on his head and asked Satan to be gone and for God to fill him up! I prayed for his spirit to soften, his mood to lighten and his attitude to change. He looked at me with wide eyes the entire time and when I said AMEN, I gave him a huge hug and told him I loved him.

We did not go from that moment to him becoming the perfect, obedient child. But we did see a change in him from that moment. A light came into his eyes that has not left. Is he still defiant and disobedient at times? Sure. But, do I have hope? You betcha! I can pull out that Bible at any time and read God's word over him or over anything! God's word is alive and active, sharper than any sword! And it NEVER comes back void.

> ### *REFLECTION QUESTION*
>
> What truth do you need to pray over your children today?

Day 25

When Life Gives You Lemons...

You intended to harm me, but God intended it all for good.

GENESIS 50:20

Life certainly likes to give us lemons sometimes. What we do with those lemons will determine what happens next.

When I was working at a top-energy company in our state, I did not yet have kids but we were happily married and life was good. When I got pregnant, I knew I wanted to get into a profession that allowed me to make my own schedule and be a present Mom. I was not ready to leave my full-time profession and the security is provided but knew that I hated what I was doing at the time. It was not a good fit for me and my boss was downright mean! I went back to work after maternity leave and I was miserable to say the least. But I kept going and working. At the same time, I decided to pursue my real estate license. After passing my state test, I knew I wanted to get started but did not have extra time since I still worked full-time. After returning back to work for 30 days, I was suddenly let go from the energy company. I was devastated, scared and unsure of the future. But...God was not. He took that broken and defeated young woman and turned me into who I am today. He picked up the broken pieces and created something new and meaningful again. And it was a future that was even better than I had ever planned!

If I had not been let go at that time, I would have stayed in comfort but unhappiness. God graciously removed me and put me on a new path. I am so glad for His provision, even when it hurt. I am now exactly where I need to be and I am thankful that God lead the way! Bye, bye, mean boss. Now I get to be my own boss!

Course-correcting is a part of life. Nothing rarely goes as we planned it to go, unfortunately. When we get lemons thrown at us, how quickly can we turn them into lemonade by adding water and a whole lotta sugar?

REFLECTION QUESTION

What area of your life did the enemy try to steal? How can God reverse it for His good and glory?

Day 26

You Cannot Have a Testimony Without a Test

Jesus answered, "It is written: 'Man shall not live on bread alone, but on every word that comes from the mouth of God.'

MATTHEW 4:4

According to the dictionary, a testimony is "firsthand authentication of a fact". When you share a testimony, you have witnessed something in person, having attested to what it looked like, felt like, sounded like. You were there and there is no denying that fact. Before we can have a testimony, something has to happen worth testifying about. Often times, it is a test. A test gives us room for a testimony to develop.

Wouldn't it be great if we gained wisdom without actual trials? Wouldn't it be nice if we knew at 16 what we know at 40? What I wouldn't give to go back and shake my teenage self! However, it does not work that way! And God tells us many times in scripture that we cannot dwell on the past. Each day is a new day! Lessons learned along the way prepare us for what is to come and equip us to better handle the opportunities and circumstances as they come along!

God allowed Jesus to be tested again and again before his true ministry began. Perhaps, He wanted Him to be rid of selfish pride and ambition. Perhaps, He wanted Him to be so dependent on His Father that He couldn't be swayed to the left or the right when trouble came. God knew the trouble that was waiting around the corner. He allowed Jesus to be put to the test. To go without food and water for forty days, to be at the end of His rope - so that He could ultimately be saved. Maybe God does the same thing for us. I have heard the phrase "You can't have a testimony without a test". During my time of struggle, it hit me like a ton of bricks! I know that hard times make strong people. But I didn't know how true it was until God allowed me to be tested. Through struggle, temptation and defeat, we can be prepared for something greater!

REFLECTION QUESTION

Write down your testimony. What tests have you faced along the way that impacted your testimony?

Day 27

Broken Bowls Lined With Gold

For you are saved by grace through faith, and this is not from yourselves; it is God's gift — not from works, so that no one can boast. For we are his workmanship, created in Christ Jesus for good works, which God prepared ahead of time for us to do.

EPHESIANS 2:8-10

I had a friend buy me a beautiful dish that had cracks throughout it. What made it unique was that these cracks were filled in with gold paint. It was a gorgeous creation and the meaning behind the pottery is even more special (Thank you, Robyn).

In traditional Japanese aesthetics, **wabi-sabi** is a world view centered on the acceptance of transience and imperfection. The aesthetic is sometimes described as one of appreciating beauty that is "imperfect, impermanent, and incomplete" in nature.

When I read about what the practice meant, it literally blew me away! After going through a hard time, we often feel that way, don't we? Incomplete? Imperfect? Does that ring a bell with you? It sure strikes a chord with me! After dealing with hurt, it's easy to feel raw, exposed and brittle.

This beautiful piece showed me that it's okay to feel this way. God can take that hurt, those cracks, those imperfections and use them for His glory! He can take our mess and work in the midst of it. Actually, I think He loves to do so! He enjoys doing a work in us, so that no one can boast, because only through Him could it be done. He makes beauty from the ashes. He turns rags into riches. He takes broken pieces and makes beautiful things. That's how my God works.

If you are hurting or have been through hurt in the past, allow God to use that situation for His purpose. Allow Him to line your cracks with gold. If we use our circumstances to give Him glory, He can make us better than new. In fact, we may even be more beautiful because of the cracks. Just like that Japanese pottery.

> ### REFLECTION QUESTION
>
> How can God take your broken pieces and use them for a beautiful purpose?

Day 28

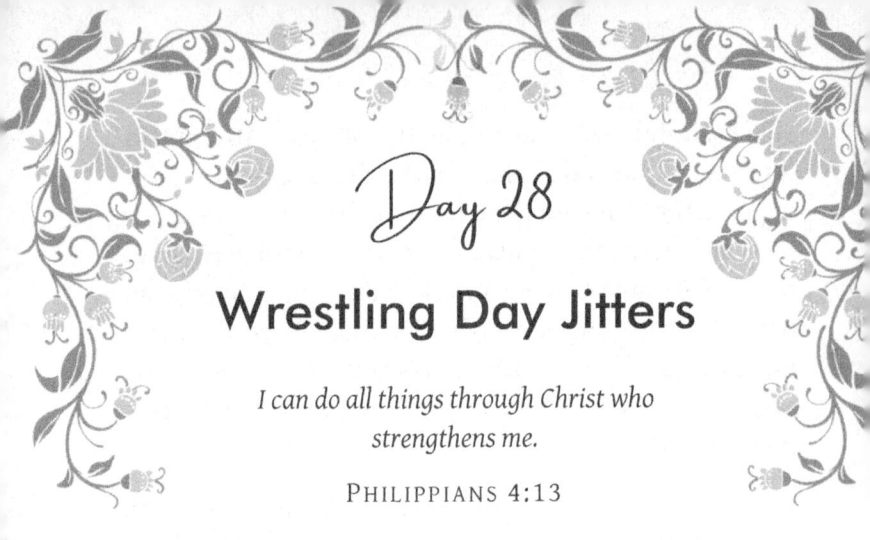

Wrestling Day Jitters

I can do all things through Christ who strengthens me.

PHILIPPIANS 4:13

My boys wrestle competitively. So between the months of November-February, you can count on us being in a gym each Saturday. The boys have been outstanding in this sport and learned very quickly! While they have earned several medals by competing over the last couple of years, each match takes a tremendous amount of strength and courage. My 7-year-old gets nervous before his first match each tournament. He starts saying things like "My stomach feels funny. I'm scared. I don't wanna go out there today." I used to get worried that maybe something was wrong with him, until I learned that his ailment always went away after that first match was completed. Once he got that first match under his belt, his whole language changed. He began saying "I'm so excited! I'm ready to get another medal! I'm strong!" All are true statements and they were true both before and after that first match! The difference maker was his mindset.

Mindset is such a powerful thing. The power of a made-up mind produces super strength! We simply must decide if we want to make up our mind to succeed or to be afraid. The problem with fear is that it can lead to paralysis, which can lead to stagnation. As a Mom, I know that success is on the other side of my boys when they wrestle! I know that they have to push past their fear in order to get to the other side and feel the joy of overcoming! I also know that it's not easy, it is scary and nobody else can do it for them.

When those jitters come, it is good to evaluate where they are coming from. Is the Holy Spirit telling you to stop? Or is fear rearing its ugly head and causing paralysis? If that is the case, I urge you not to let fear win. Because fear is a liar. And on the other side of fear lies victory.

> **REFLECTION QUESTION**
>
> What fear are you living with that you can overcome with faith?

Day 29

A'int That Just Like God?

And are justified by his grace as a gift, through the redemption that is in Christ Jesus, whom God put forward as a propitiation by his blood, to be received by faith. This was to show God's righteousness, because in his divine forbearance he had passed over former sins. It was to show his righteousness at the present time, so that he might be just and the justifier of the one who has faith in Jesus.

ROMANS 3:24-26

A little over a year after starting my own brokerage, God blessed me with the opportunity to be nominated for a big award in the industry. Not only did he graciously place me on the cover of one of the top magazines in our area, he then allowed me to be nominated to be the Cover Story of the Year. In the article, I told my story of how the brokerage began, what my background was as a woman, mom and real estate broker and owner. I was real, raw and quick to give God the glory! A little over a year after one of the darkest seasons of my life, I was standing on a stage accepting an award for being the Cover Story of the Year.

Ironically, I had some friends there with me who had stuck by my side throughout the difficult season that night. One looked at me and said with a smile and said "A'int that just like God"? (Thank you Ryan. I'll always remember this.)

He didn't have to put me in that room. He didn't have to allow me to be on that magazine or be nominated for that award or to be selected the winner. This world is superficial and awards do not matter in Heaven. But God loves us and He is faithful. And sometimes he throws us into the spotlight just because He can.

I'll never forget how that felt for my story to be redeemed. How it felt to go from defeat to soaring! I will treasure that night and that feeling. Not because of what I did. Because on my own, I am ordinary at best. But, when I allow God to work through me, awesome things happen.

REFLECTION QUESTION

How has God redeemed your story? If He has not yet, how can He in the future?

Day 30

"You Look Happy"

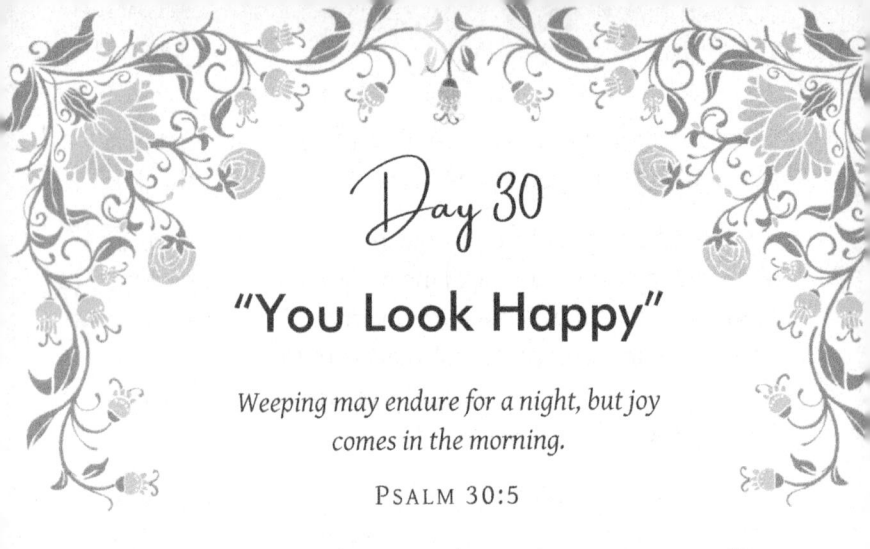

Weeping may endure for a night, but joy comes in the morning.

PSALM 30:5

My husband saw a picture of me today. I was in my office, greeting a new agent signing on and I was smiling. I was truly happy and mostly, I was proud. He saw the picture on social media and said "You look happier than I have ever seen you look". Wow! When someone you are closer to than anyone in your life tells you that, it's pretty profound. Because they know what you have been through. They know what it took to get where you are today.

I took that moment to really think about his words. They were true, I was happy. But, more than that, I felt joy over all God had given me. The road to get to a place of happiness was not easy. It was a lot of work and some days were discouraging (and honestly, some days are still bumpy). His words however, were accurate. You could see the joy in my eyes, just looking at that photo. And not only could I see it, I felt it.

What a blessing it is to be on the other side! How wonderful to see the light at the end of the tunnel! God was gracious in allowing me to come through the darkness quickly. I know in many cases, it takes more time to see that light coming in. Sometimes, it is important to just take a moment and reflect on how far God has brought you.

Maybe you are not through the trial yet. Maybe you're still in the middle. God has purpose in your pain. You can be assured that if your joy rests in the Lord, you will never be defeated.

> ### REFLECTION QUESTION
>
> Where are you in your journey? Can you see the purpose behind the pain?

Choose Your Hard

Forgiving is hard.
Being miserable is harder.
Choose your hard.

Taking chances is hard.
Having regrets is harder.
Choose your hard.

Moving forward is hard.
Feeling stuck is harder.
Choose your hard.

Chasing your dreams is hard.
Realizing you never tried is harder.
Choose your hard.

Starting fresh is hard.
Sitting in complacency is harder.
Choose your hard.

Following God is hard.
Not having God by your side is harder.
Choose your hard.

Hard is a choice. It's not easy, but it's worth it.
Choose hard today.

WRITTEN BY ASHLEY SCHUBERT, FEBRUARY 2023

THANK YOU

Thank you for reading "Joy in the Weeds". I pray that as you read, you were able to feel the love and the goodness of God throughout the pages. I pray that you were encouraged to forgive, dream again and maintain joy along the journey. If you do not yet have a relationship with Jesus, I would love to send you a Bible. Please e-mail me at AshleyM.Schubert@gmail.com with BIBLE in the subject line, include your address in the body and share a little of your story with me. If you have not yet given your life to Jesus, I can assure you that it will be the best decision you will ever make! God is good all the time, even when life is not. I would also be happy to pray with you and for you if you'll email me with the word PRAYER in the subject line.

I hope this book has inspired you to find joy in your current situation, even if it feels as though the weeds are tall and thick. With God by your side, the future is limitless. And only He can provide true joy.

Blessings,

Ashley

LET'S CONNECT ON INSTAGRAM:
AshleySchubert_Speaks

IF YOU ENJOYED THIS BOOK, I HOPE YOU WILL CHECK OUT MY OTHERS ON AMAZON:

Raising A Business And Babies
30 Days To Shine
OverRated

And please leave a review on Amazon so that others can find the book, just like you did!

SPECIAL THANKS

To my Husband: Thank you for believing in me, pushing me and loving me. I have learned that when you tell me I cannot do things, it is only because you know I can and will! I am thankful for your continued urging to stay consistently on my course. You have been a friend through it all. I am so glad God gave me you on this journey and that he has blessed us with our crazy life!

To my Kids: I pray every morning that you will be a light for Jesus wherever you go! If I can do one thing right, it would be to show you how much Jesus loves you! Your Bible is your truth and your sword. Remember the words and use them as you grow. I will always be your biggest fan, no matter what you choose to do! I will do my best to model what a strong Christian woman, wife and mother look like. And where I fail, I pray you give me the grace to pick up and try again. I am blessed and thankful to be your Mommy and that God gave us all of you!

To my parents: Thanks for throwing me up on a stage to sing from the time I was two-years-old. Thanks for chasing me all over the country to watch me on the basketball court. Thanks for believing in me, always. Thanks for modeling what a Godly marriage looks like! Thanks for family dinners around the table each night. Thanks for showing me what hard work looks like. Thanks for never making church optional. Thanks for teaching me to love Jesus. I am forever thankful for your love.

To my family and friends: Thanks for walking beside me in great times and in hard times. I appreciate your support and love! Thanks for allowing me to be myself, to live authentically and for appreciating the beautifully chaotic life I have built.

To my editing team: Thank you for pouring through these pages, making edits and taking the time to help me make this devotional the best it can be! I appreciate you.

To God: And to God almighty, may you get the glory for every good thing in my life. May my life be a light that shines brightly for you in all that I do. May I become less so that you may become greater. Thank you for the gifts and abilities you have given me. Now, I surrender them to you.

Made in the USA
Middletown, DE
10 July 2024